The Neo-Babylonian Empire

Kelly Daniels

Series Editor **Rob Waring**

Level 4 - ❸

The Neo-Babylonian Empire

Kelly Daniels

© 2017 Seed Learning, Inc.

Series Editor: Rob Waring
Acquisitions Editor: Liana Robinson
Copy Editor: Casey Malarcher
Cover/Interior Design: Andy Roh

ISBN: 978-1-9464-5232-0

10 9 8 7 6 5 4 3 2 1
21 20 19 18 17

Contents

Empires Come and Go

When you think of great empires of the past, you probably think of Greece, Egypt, and Rome. All of these were certainly great empires of the past. But there were other empires of the Near East long ago that were also important.

The lands of the Near East changed hands many times among the ancient empires. The countries that are Turkey, Syria, Iraq, and Iran had many different rulers. In fact, the empire of Babylon ruled part of these lands from around 1900-1600 BC.

An old map showing the Near East, Middle East, and Far East

4

One of the ancient kings of Babylon was Hammurabi. He wrote laws for the people to follow. These laws were recorded in stone, so we can still read them today. They are the famous laws of Hammurabi's Code.

After three hundred years, the ancient empire of Babylon fell. Then another empire, the Assyrian Empire, rose in power in the Near East.

The Assyrian Empire was very strong for a long time. But like all empires, it could not last forever. It came to an end around 600 BC when Babylon returned to power.

Assyrian warriors

Hammurabi's Code in the British Museum, London

Babylon Rises Again

At first, the Assyrians controlled the lands in the northern part of the Near East. Over time, they expanded their empire to the south and took control of the city of Babylon. Because the Assyrian Empire was so big, there were many kings across the empire. These kings ruled small parts of the empire, but they had to follow the orders of the empire's Assyrian king.

The Assyrian Empire grew and grew.

Assyrian Empire – 824 B.C.
Assyrian Empire – 671 B.C.

The writing on this ancient object has Nabopolassar's name on it.

In 626 BC, a new king took control in Babylon. His name was Nabopolassar, and he was tired of living under Assyrian rule. Nabopolassar led the people of Babylon in a war against Assyria, and he won! Then in 612 BC, he won an even bigger battle against Assyria. The Babylonian Empire was beginning to grow.

King Nabopolassar

A view of the ancient city of Babylon

Babylon's Great King

Nebuchadnezzar's court

In 605 BC, Nabopolassar's son became the next king of Babylon. His name was Nebuchadnezzar, and he was the most famous king of the Neo-Babylonian Empire.

The empire was quite large!

Like his father, Nebuchadnezzar was good at leading the people in war. He expanded Babylon's empire north and west. The Babylonian army usually moved people out of the new lands that were conquered as the empire grew. The Assyrians usually did this, too. The reason the king wanted to do this was to keep the people in fear. It also made it harder for people from the new land to get together again and fight against the king.

The Burning of Jerusalem by Nebuchadnezzar's Army painted by Juan de la Corte

One of the cities that Nebuchadnezzar took was Jerusalem. This was the most important city of the Jewish people in the Near East. When Nebuchadnezzar took Jerusalem in 586 BC, he ordered thousands of Jewish people there to move to Babylon where they lived as slaves. One young man at the time was named Daniel. This

A stone marking the boundary of Babylon's empire

was the same Daniel who wrote one of the books of the Bible which tells about life in Babylon at the court of King Nebuchadnezzar.

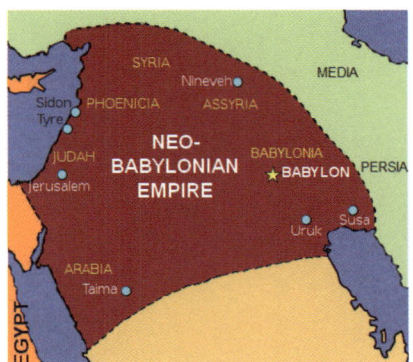

The Neo-Babylonian Empire

The Wonders of Babylon

King Nebuchadnezzar was not just a good fighter. He was also a king who dreamed of making Babylon a great and beautiful city.

Restored ruins of ancient Babylon, Iraq

Nebuchadnezzar ordered the damaged wall around the city to be built again, better than before. This wall kept the people inside the city safe. But Nebuchadnezzar didn't want this city wall to be just like the walls of other cities.

He had special gates built, too. One of these gates was the Ishtar Gate, named after the goddess Ishtar. The gate was built with special blue stone and had pictures of cows and lions on it. Visitors to the city saw this beautiful gate as they entered.

A copy of the Ishtar Gate, Iraq

The wall around Babylon

Nebuchadnezzar Ordering the Building of the Hanging Gardens by Rene-Antoine Houasse

A ziggurat

But the wonders of Babylon did not stop at the city's Ishtar Gate. Inside the city, Nebuchadnezzar had a huge ziggurat built. This was a temple to the Babylonian god Marduk. The actual temple was at the top of the ziggurat, 90 m above the city!

If the temple of Marduk failed to impress visitors, then the king's Hanging Gardens certainly would. Although Greek visitors to the city wrote about the wonderful Hanging Gardens of Babylon, there is still some question today about if they were real. From the Greek writers, we read that the gardens grew on balconies above the city streets. The highest balcony was over 20 m above the street, but plants grew on lower balconies as well.

The writing on this object describes Nebuchadnezzar's building projects.

The Hanging Gardens, a gift for a queen

According to legend, Nebuchadnezzar built the gardens for one of his wives. She came from a green land with many plants, but Babylon wasn't like that. The Hanging Gardens were built to help her remember her faraway home.

During his 43 years as king, Nebuchadnezzar built palaces, bridges, and more!

A drawing of Nebuchadnezzar

City Life

Although the city of Babylon was filled with wonders, it was not wonderful for everyone there. Probably about 200,000 people lived in Babylon. The city was full of people, and it was dirty. During the long, hot summers, it must have smelled terrible!

A slave of the ancient Near East

All around the city, farmers grew things that people in the city needed. However, the farmers did not live outside the city near their fields. They had homes inside the city walls.

Maybe this is what visitors saw as they came near the city.

A typical house in the city of Babylon had three floors, but the house was not large. It was tall and thin. The streets between the houses were thin as well. People threw all of their garbage out into the streets beside or in front of their houses.

One way that the leaders of the city "cleaned" the dirty streets was by covering the streets with clay. This made the whole street higher. Sometimes it was a problem for people to go in and out of their front doors when the streets got higher. Then they had to cut openings down to their doors.

Or they could build steps up and make new doors on a higher floor of their house.

People threw out dirty water and garbage onto the streets of the city.

A New Empire Rises

A carving of Amel Merodach and a king under his control

Nebuchadnezzar was king of Babylon for 43 years. He expanded the empire that his father left him and made Babylon one of the greatest cities of that age. When he died, his son, Amel Merodach (also called "Evil Merodach") became king.

Amel Merodach was not a great king. In fact, he only ruled for three years. Then in the three years after that, two more kings led the empire. One of these was a child! As you might guess, the Babylonian Empire was in trouble.

A wall carving of the great king Nebuchadnezzar

An image of Marduk taken from a stone carving in Babylon

In 556 BC, the last king of Babylon came to power. His name was Nabonidus (also called Nabu-Na'id). He was probably a son-in-law of Nebuchadnezzar. He was made king after some trouble in the city caused by the priests of Marduk. During his time as king, Nabonidus spent years away from Babylon. His son, Belshazzar, served as co-king in the city.

Together, Nabonidus and his son led the empire for 14 years.

A carving of Nabonidus in the British Museum, London

The writing on this ancient object has Nabonidus's name on it.

To the north of Babylon, Persia was growing in power. The king of Persia, Cyrus the Great, came down and captured Babylon in 539 BC. He killed Belshazzar, but no one really knows what happened to Nabonidus.

However, one thing is clear. The fall of Babylon to Cyrus the Great brought an end to the Neo-Babylonian Empire.

Tourists can visit the tomb of Cyrus the Great in Iran.

King Cyrus the Great

Cyrus let many slaves in Babylon return to their homelands.

Comprehension Questions

1. The lands of the Near East include…
   (a) Iraq.
   (b) Syria.
   (c) Turkey.
   (d) All of the above

2. Hammurabi is known for making…
   (a) a set of laws.
   (b) a temple of stone.
   (c) the city of Babylon.
   (d) All of the above

3. What did Nabopolassar do?
   (a) Wrote a code
   (b) Fought the Babylonians
   (c) Fought the Assyrians
   (d) Married a goddess

4. Who was Nebuchadnezzar?
   (a) Assyria's last king
   (b) A priest of Marduk
   (c) Nabopolassar's son
   (d) All of the above

5. Which famous city fell to Babylon in 586 BC?
   (a) Rome
   (b) Jerusalem
   (c) Cairo
   (d) Athens

6. Which wonder of Babylon was made of blue stone?
   (a) Babylon's city wall
   (b) The king's palace
   (c) The Ishtar Gate
   (d) The Temple of Marduk

7. The tallest thing found in Babylon was…
   (a) the king's palace.
   (b) the city wall.
   (c) the Hanging Gardens.
   (d) a ziggurat.

8. Which is true about the city of Babylon?
   (a) It was not crowded.
   (b) Houses there had no doors.
   (c) No garbage was on the streets.
   (d) It was very dirty.

9. Who was king of Babylon the longest?
   (a) Nebuchadnezzar
   (b) Amel Merodach
   (c) Nabonidus
   (d) Belshazzar

10. The Babylonian Empire fell to…
    (a) the Assyrians.
    (b) the Egyptians.
    (c) the Persians.
    (d) the Romans.

Key 1. (d) 2. (a) 3. (c) 4. (c) 5. (b) 6. (c) 7. (d) 8. (d) 9. (a) 10. (c)

Glossary

- **ancient** very old

- **balcony** a place on the outside of a building above the first floor where a person can stand

- **battle** a big fight between two groups of soldiers

- **capture** to catch someone and make them your prisoner

- **clay** a kind of soil that can be shaped by hand when it is wet, used for pots, bricks, etc.

- **conquer** to take control of a country or defeat people in a war

- **empire** a group of countries ruled by one person or government

- **expand** to make larger and/or wider

- **faraway** very far; in the distance

- **goddess** a female god

- **legend** an old story people tell about a person or event

- **palace** a large home for a king or queen

- **priest** a person who can lead or perform religious ceremonies

- **slave** a person who is bought and owned by another person

- **temple** a place for religious worship and sacrifice

- **ziggurat** a temple built like a pyramid with a path for walking up and down that goes around the outside of the structure

World History Timeline

This chart shows a rough overview of world history.
Some of the dates have been simplified.

World History Timeline

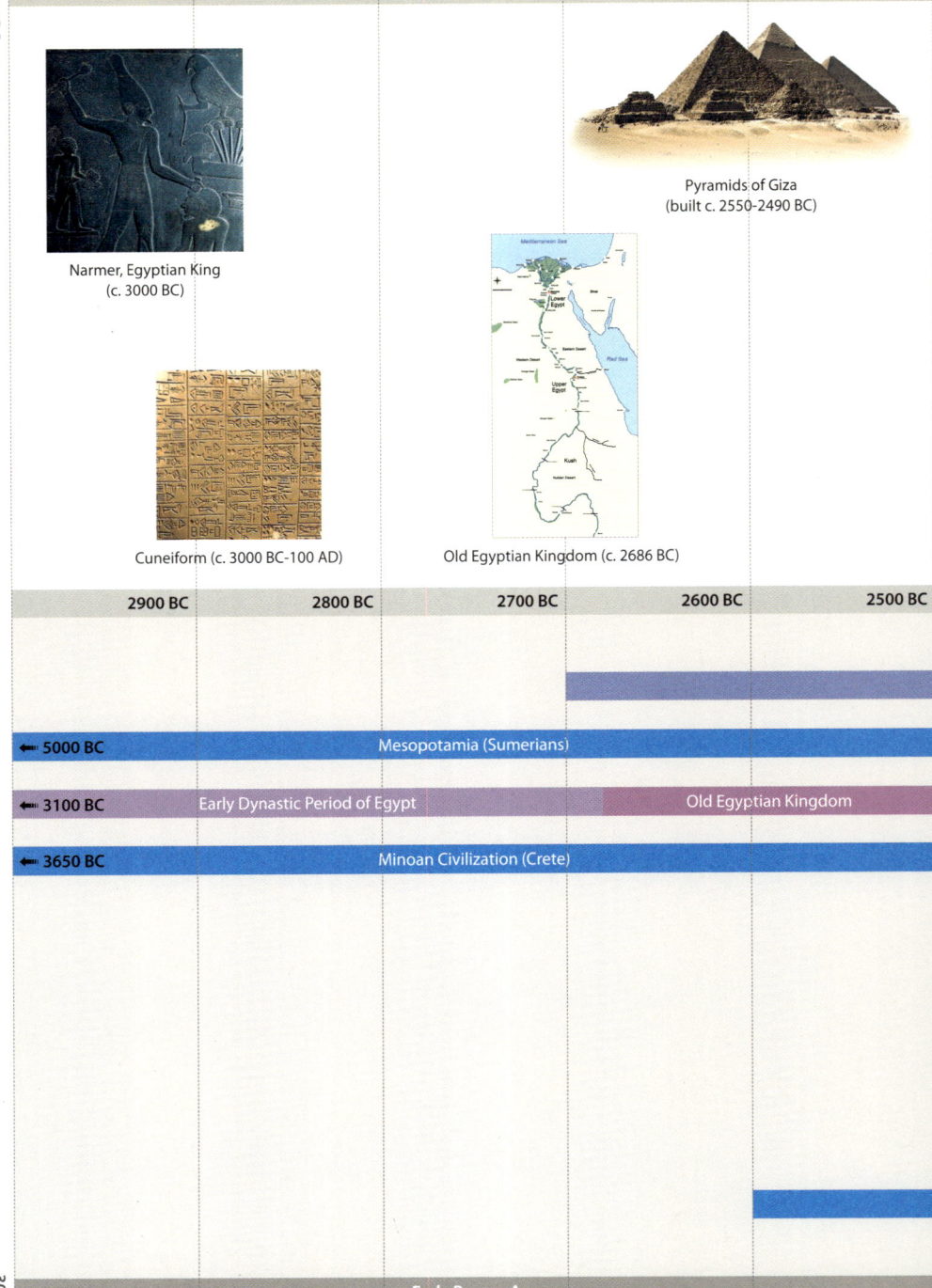

| 2900 BC | 2800 BC | 2700 BC | 2600 BC | 2500 BC |

Pyramids of Giza
(built c. 2550-2490 BC)

Narmer, Egyptian King
(c. 3000 BC)

Cuneiform (c. 3000 BC-100 AD)

Old Egyptian Kingdom (c. 2686 BC)

| 2900 BC | 2800 BC | 2700 BC | 2600 BC | 2500 BC |

⟵ 5000 BC   Mesopotamia (Sumerians)

⟵ 3100 BC   Early Dynastic Period of Egypt   Old Egyptian Kingdom

⟵ 3650 BC   Minoan Civilization (Crete)

Early Bronze Age

| 2900 BC | 2800 BC | 2700 BC | 2600 BC | 2500 BC |

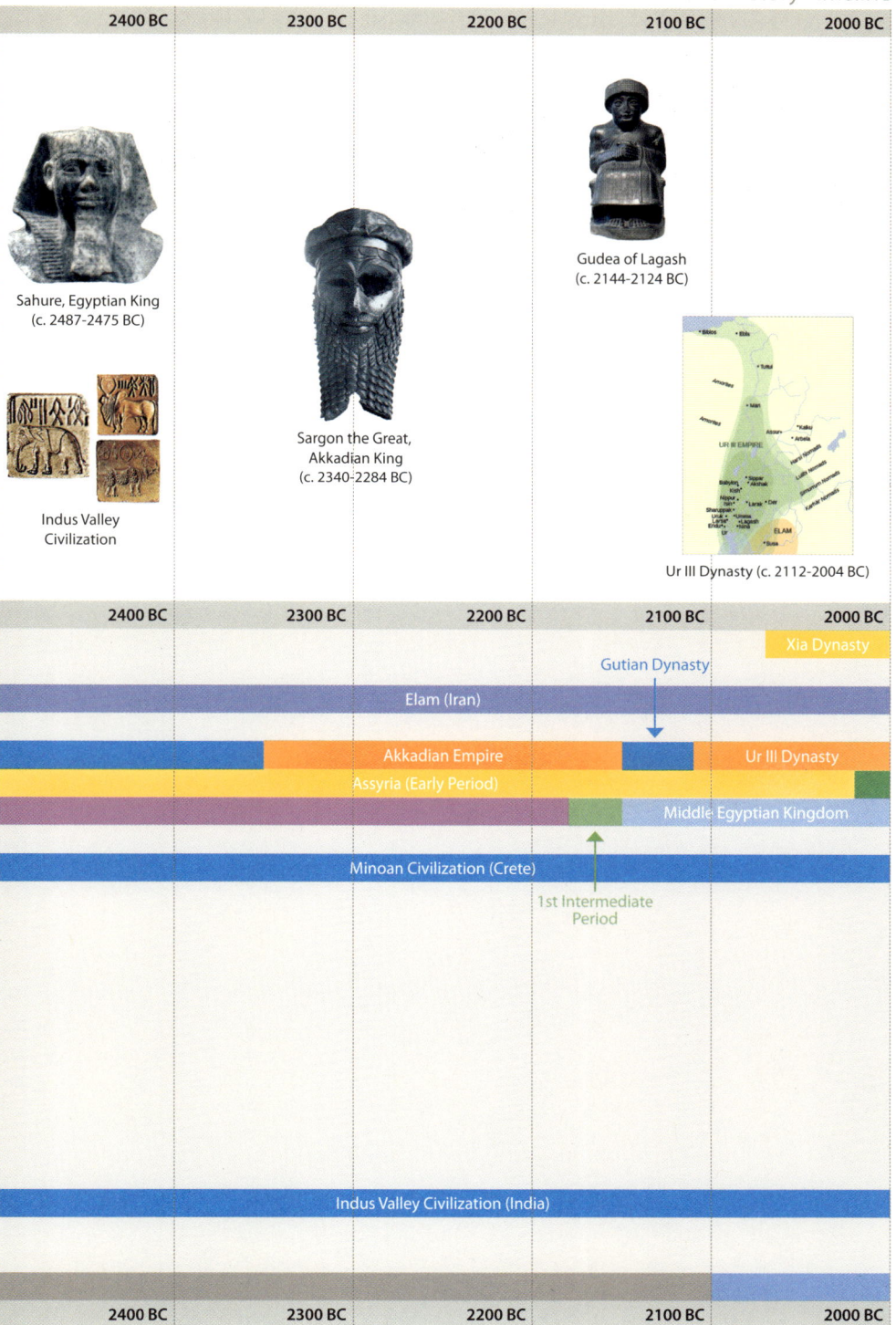

2400 BC	2300 BC	2200 BC	2100 BC	2000 BC

Sahure, Egyptian King
(c. 2487-2475 BC)

Indus Valley
Civilization

Sargon the Great,
Akkadian King
(c. 2340-2284 BC)

Gudea of Lagash
(c. 2144-2124 BC)

UR III EMPIRE

ELAM

Ur III Dynasty (c. 2112-2004 BC)

2400 BC	2300 BC	2200 BC	2100 BC	2000 BC

Xia Dynasty

Gutian Dynasty

Elam (Iran)

Akkadian Empire

Ur III Dynasty

Assyria (Early Period)

Middle Egyptian Kingdom

Minoan Civilization (Crete)

1st Intermediate
Period

Indus Valley Civilization (India)

2400 BC	2300 BC	2200 BC	2100 BC	2000 BC

World History Timeline

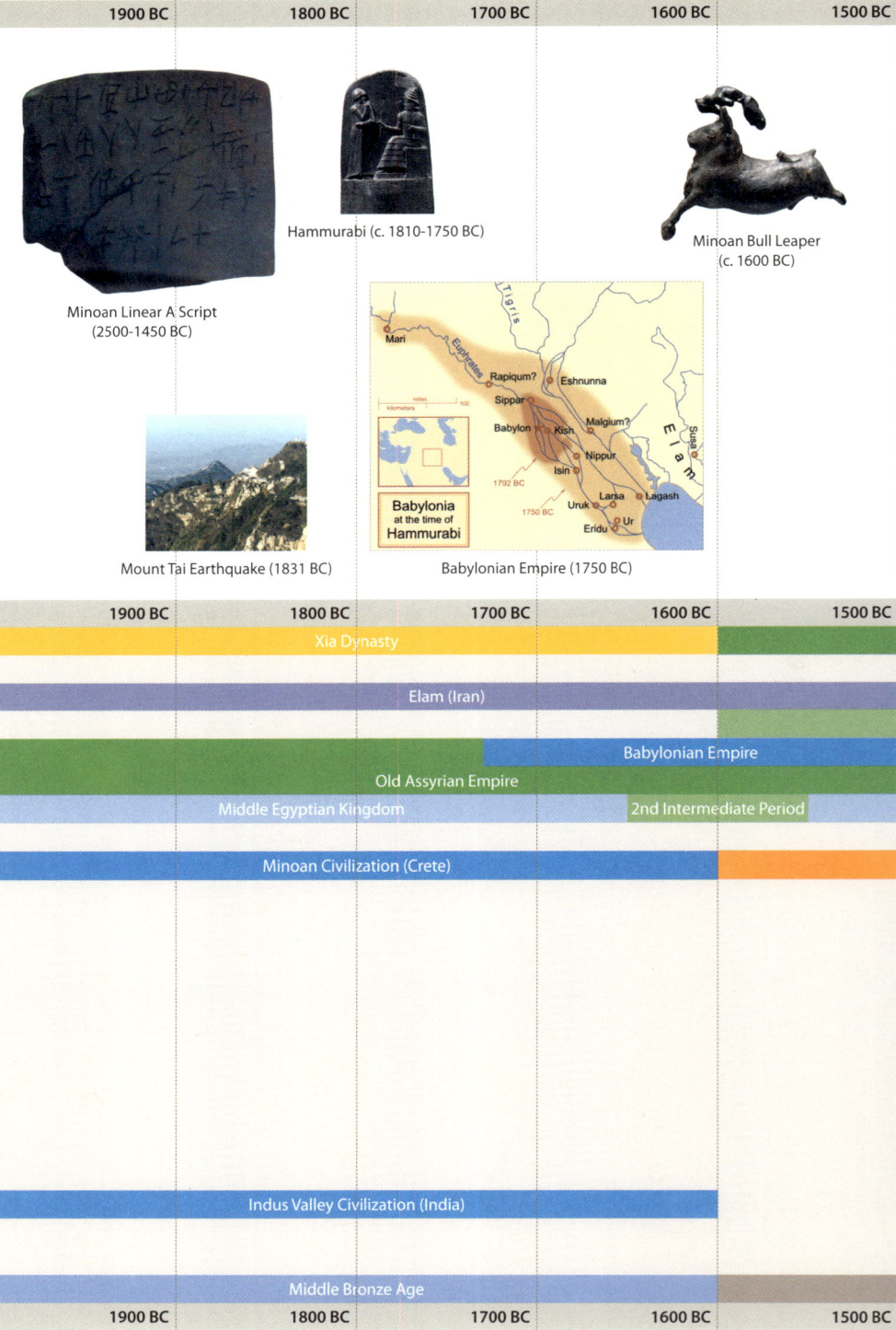

1900 BC	1800 BC	1700 BC	1600 BC	1500 BC

Hammurabi (c. 1810-1750 BC)

Minoan Bull Leaper (c. 1600 BC)

Minoan Linear A Script (2500-1450 BC)

Mount Tai Earthquake (1831 BC)

Babylonian Empire (1750 BC)

Mari
Euphrates
Tigris
Rapiqum?
Eshnunna
Sippar
Malgium?
Babylon
Kish
Susa
Elam
Nippur
1792 BC
Isin
Larsa
Lagash
1750 BC
Uruk
Eridu
Ur

Babylonia at the time of **Hammurabi**

1900 BC	1800 BC	1700 BC	1600 BC	1500 BC

Xia Dynasty

Elam (Iran)

Babylonian Empire

Old Assyrian Empire

Middle Egyptian Kingdom

2nd Intermediate Period

Minoan Civilization (Crete)

Indus Valley Civilization (India)

Middle Bronze Age

1900 BC	1800 BC	1700 BC	1600 BC	1500 BC

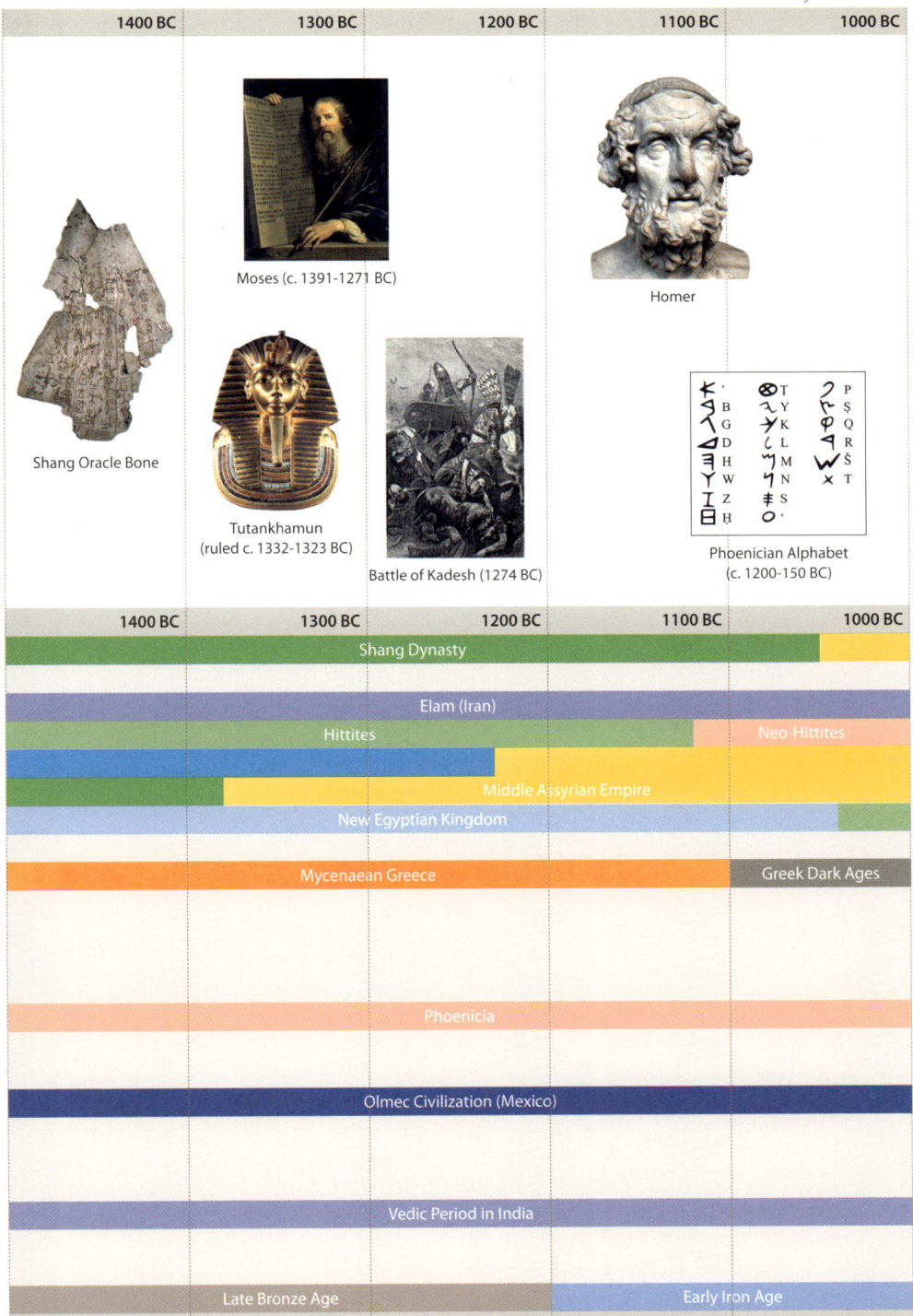

1400 BC	1300 BC	1200 BC	1100 BC	1000 BC

Moses (c. 1391-1271 BC)

Homer

Shang Oracle Bone

Tutankhamun
(ruled c. 1332-1323 BC)

Battle of Kadesh (1274 BC)

Phoenician Alphabet
(c. 1200-150 BC)

1400 BC	1300 BC	1200 BC	1100 BC	1000 BC

Shang Dynasty

Elam (Iran)

Hittites

Neo-Hittites

Middle Assyrian Empire

New Egyptian Kingdom

Mycenaean Greece

Greek Dark Ages

Phoenicia

Olmec Civilization (Mexico)

Vedic Period in India

Late Bronze Age

Early Iron Age

1400 BC	1300 BC	1200 BC	1100 BC	1000 BC

World History Timeline

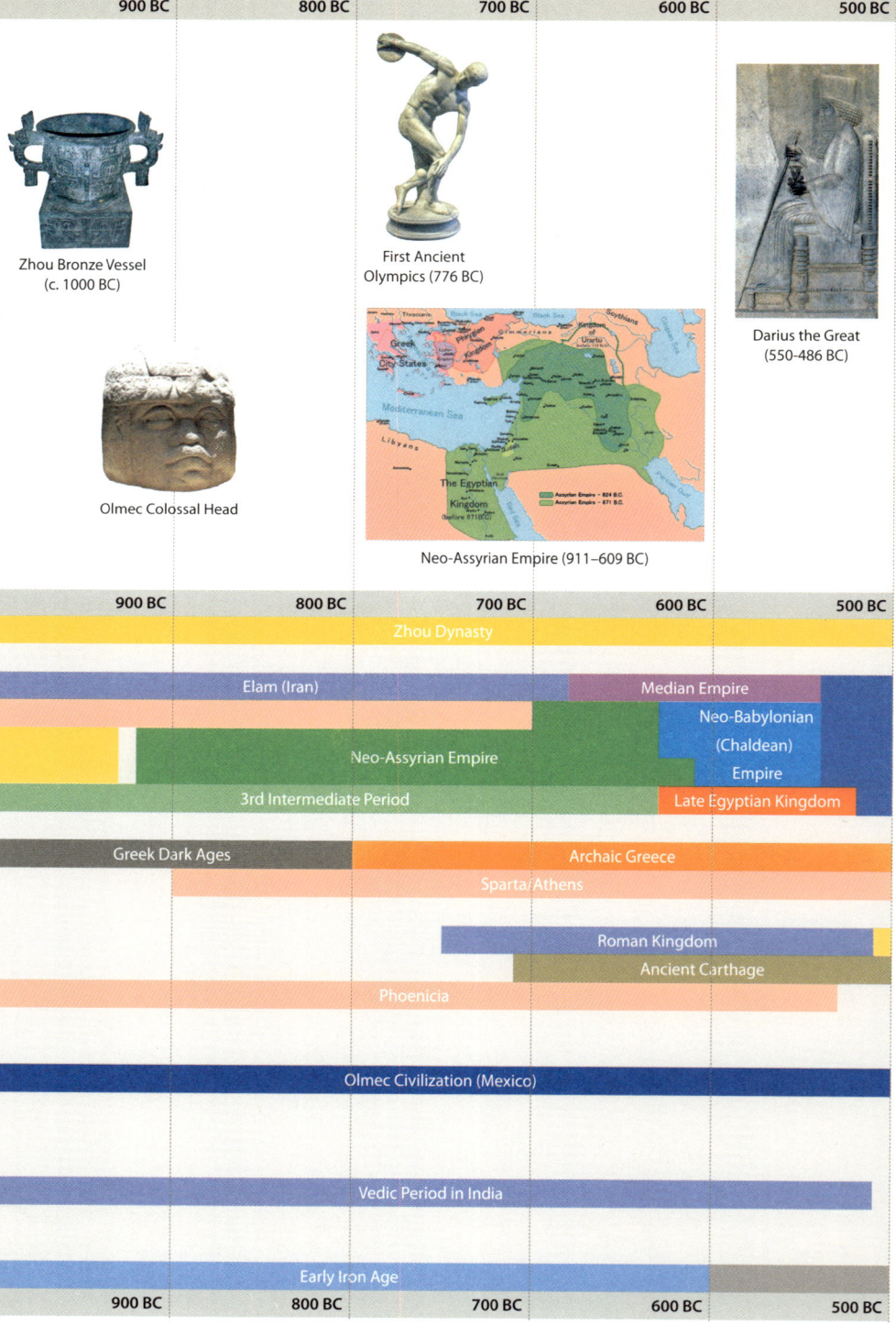

| 900 BC | 800 BC | 700 BC | 600 BC | 500 BC |

Zhou Bronze Vessel
(c. 1000 BC)

First Ancient
Olympics (776 BC)

Darius the Great
(550-486 BC)

Olmec Colossal Head

Neo-Assyrian Empire (911–609 BC)

| 900 BC | 800 BC | 700 BC | 600 BC | 500 BC |

Zhou Dynasty

Elam (Iran)

Median Empire

Neo-Babylonian (Chaldean) Empire

Neo-Assyrian Empire

3rd Intermediate Period

Late Egyptian Kingdom

Greek Dark Ages

Archaic Greece

Sparta/Athens

Roman Kingdom

Ancient Carthage

Phoenicia

Olmec Civilization (Mexico)

Vedic Period in India

Early Iron Age

| 900 BC | 800 BC | 700 BC | 600 BC | 500 BC |

| 400 BC | 300 BC | 200 BC | 100 BC | 0 |

Alexander the Great
(356–323 BC)

Julius Caesar
(100–44 BC)

Cleopatra
(69–30 BC)

Hannibal
(247–183 BC)

Battle of Salamis
(480 BC)

Seleucid Empire (312–63 BC)

Rossetta Stone
(created 196 BC)

| 400 BC | 300 BC | 200 BC | 100 BC | 0 |

Zhou Dynasty

Qin

Han Dynasty

Achaemenid (Persian) Empire

Alexander the Great

Parthian Empire

Seleucid Empire

Ptolemaic Kingdom

(Hellenistic Greece)

Roman Empire

Classical Greece

Sparta/Athens

Roman Republic

Roman Empire

Maurya Empire

Middle Iron Age

| 400 BC | 300 BC | 200 BC | 100 BC | 0 |

World History Timeline

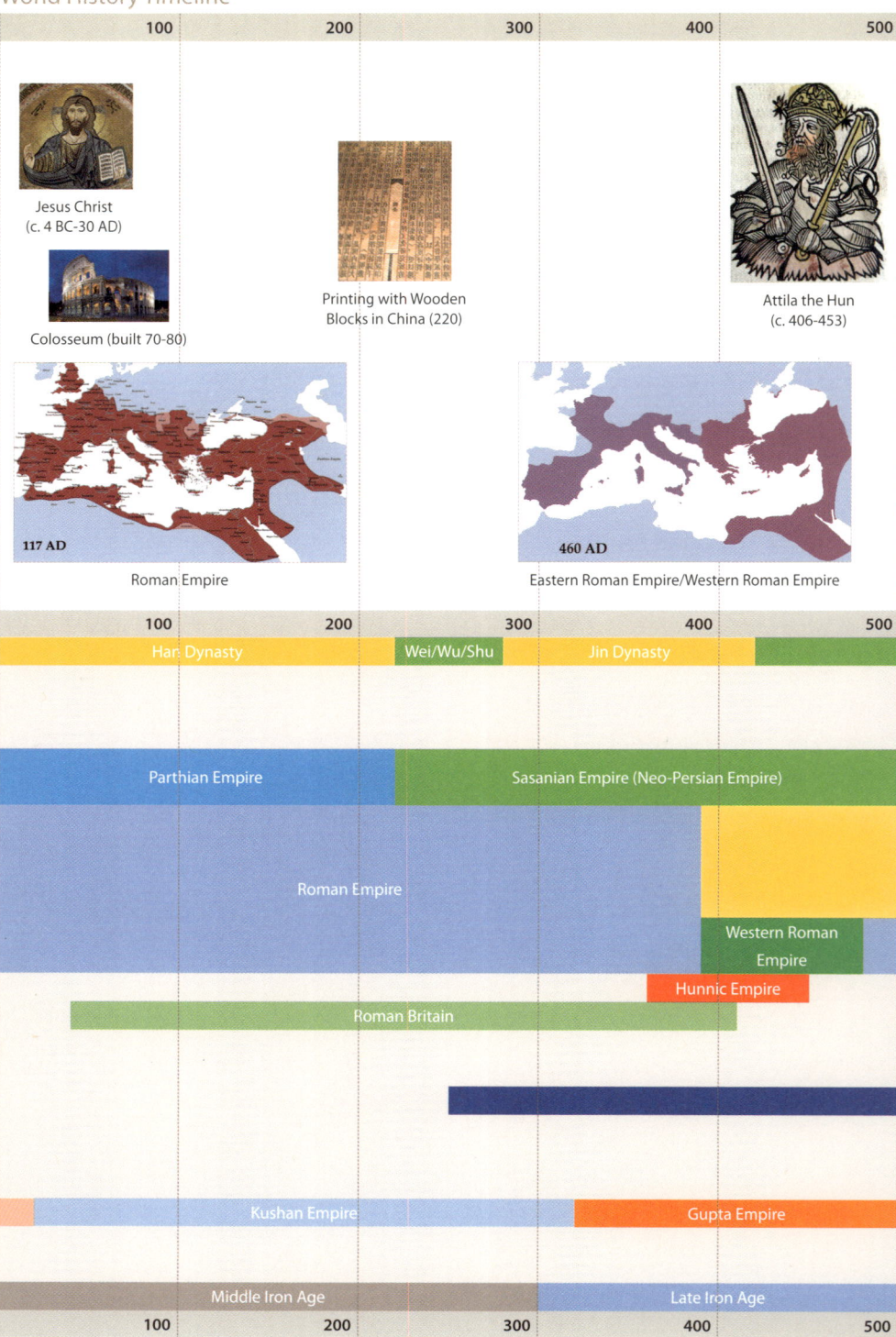

	100	200	300	400	500

Jesus Christ
(c. 4 BC-30 AD)

Colosseum (built 70-80)

Printing with Wooden
Blocks in China (220)

Attila the Hun
(c. 406-453)

117 AD

Roman Empire

460 AD

Eastern Roman Empire/Western Roman Empire

100	200	300	400	500

Han Dynasty | Wei/Wu/Shu | Jin Dynasty

Parthian Empire | Sasanian Empire (Neo-Persian Empire)

Roman Empire

Western Roman Empire

Hunnic Empire

Roman Britain

Kushan Empire | Gupta Empire

Middle Iron Age | Late Iron Age

100	200	300	400	500

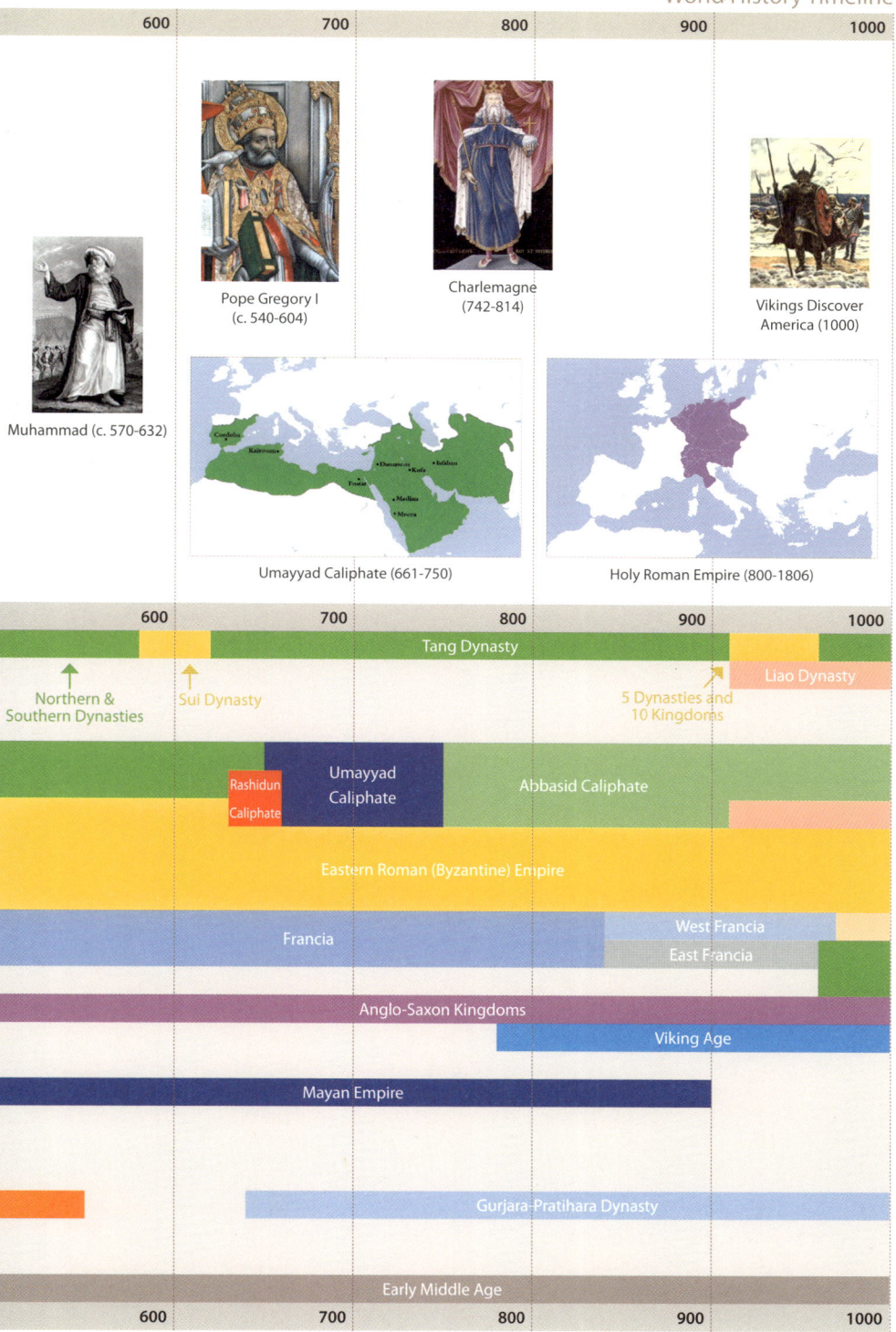

600   700   800   900   1000

Pope Gregory I
(c. 540-604)

Charlemagne
(742-814)

Vikings Discover
America (1000)

Muhammad (c. 570-632)

Umayyad Caliphate (661-750)

Holy Roman Empire (800-1806)

600   700   800   900   1000

Tang Dynasty

Liao Dynasty

Northern &
Southern Dynasties

Sui Dynasty

5 Dynasties and
10 Kingdoms

Rashidun
Caliphate

Umayyad
Caliphate

Abbasid Caliphate

Eastern Roman (Byzantine) Empire

Francia

West Francia

East Francia

Anglo-Saxon Kingdoms

Viking Age

Mayan Empire

Gurjara-Pratihara Dynasty

Early Middle Age

600   700   800   900   1000

World History Timeline

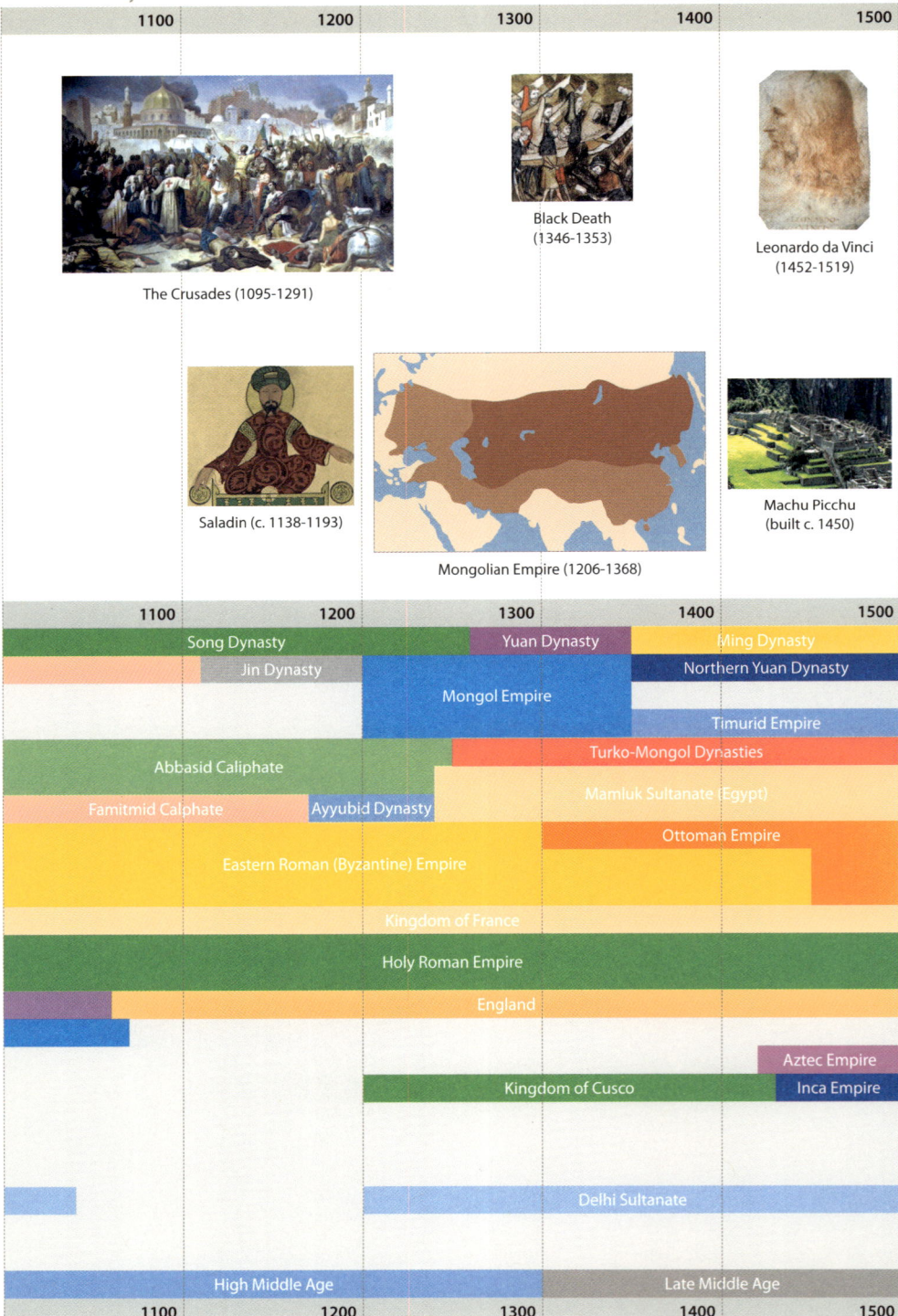

The Crusades (1095-1291)

Black Death (1346-1353)

Leonardo da Vinci (1452-1519)

Saladin (c. 1138-1193)

Mongolian Empire (1206-1368)

Machu Picchu (built c. 1450)

1100	1200	1300	1400	1500

Song Dynasty
Yuan Dynasty
Ming Dynasty
Jin Dynasty
Northern Yuan Dynasty
Mongol Empire
Timurid Empire
Abbasid Caliphate
Turko-Mongol Dynasties
Famitmid Calphate
Ayyubid Dynasty
Mamluk Sultanate (Egypt)
Ottoman Empire
Eastern Roman (Byzantine) Empire
Kingdom of France
Holy Roman Empire
England
Aztec Empire
Kingdom of Cusco
Inca Empire
Delhi Sultanate
High Middle Age
Late Middle Age

1100	1200	1300	1400	1500

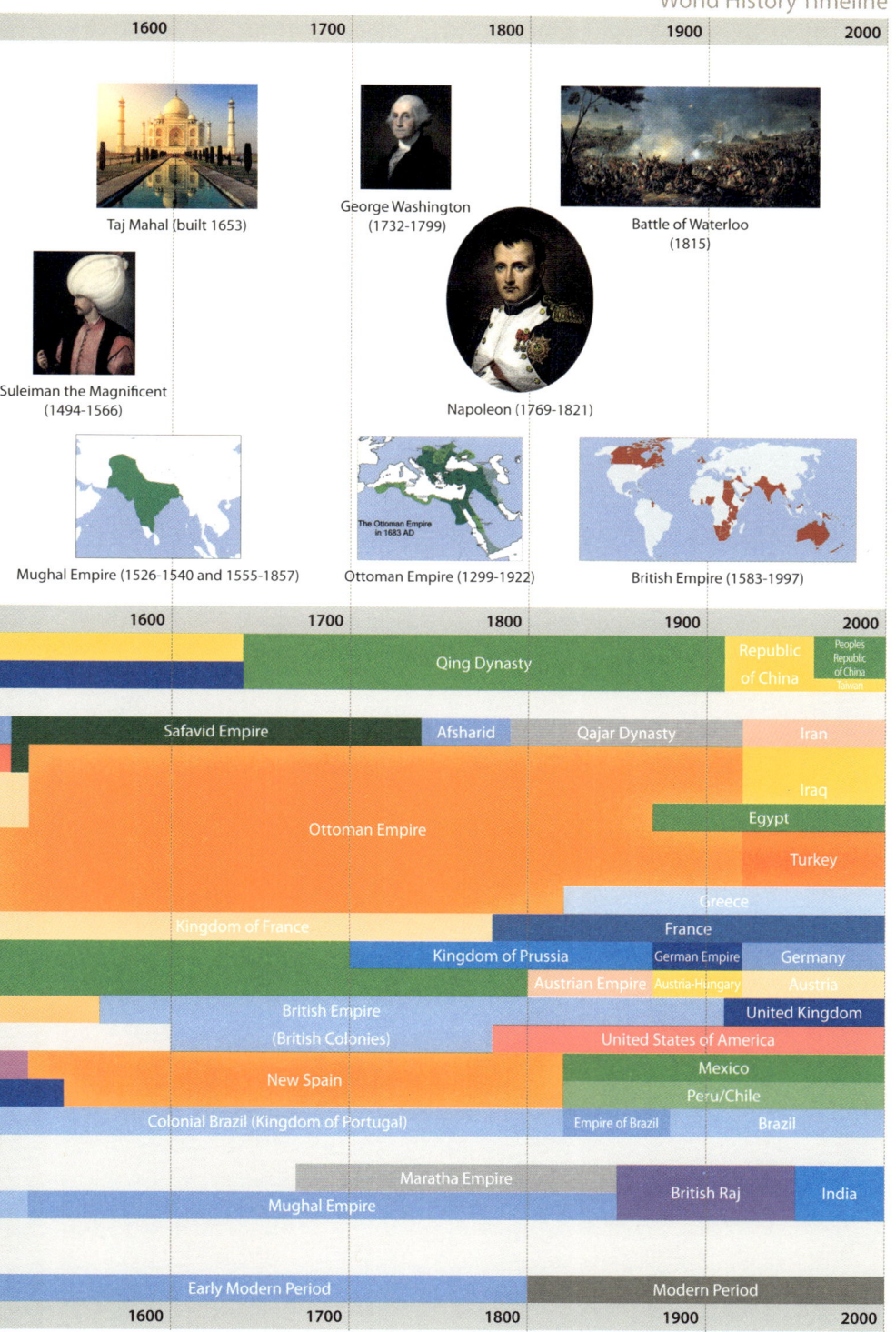

World History Timeline

| 1600 | 1700 | 1800 | 1900 | 2000 |

Taj Mahal (built 1653)

George Washington (1732-1799)

Battle of Waterloo (1815)

Suleiman the Magnificent (1494-1566)

Napoleon (1769-1821)

Mughal Empire (1526-1540 and 1555-1857)

The Ottoman Empire in 1683 AD

Ottoman Empire (1299-1922)

British Empire (1583-1997)

| 1600 | 1700 | 1800 | 1900 | 2000 |

Qing Dynasty — Republic of China — People's Republic of China / Taiwan

Safavid Empire — Afsharid — Qajar Dynasty — Iran

Ottoman Empire — Iraq — Egypt — Turkey — Greece

Kingdom of France — France

Kingdom of Prussia — German Empire — Germany

Austrian Empire — Austria-Hungary — Austria

British Empire — United Kingdom

(British Colonies) — United States of America

New Spain — Mexico — Peru/Chile

Colonial Brazil (Kingdom of Portugal) — Empire of Brazil — Brazil

Maratha Empire — British Raj — India

Mughal Empire

Early Modern Period — Modern Period

| 1600 | 1700 | 1800 | 1900 | 2000 |

List of Books